THE CHEMISTRY
OF ANGELS

THE CHEMISTRY OF ANGELS

Isobel Thrilling

halfacrown

halfacrown

First published in Great Britain in 2000
by halfacrown publishers
198 Victoria Avenue
Kingston upon Hull HU5 3DY

Printed in Great Britain by
Copytech UK, Peterborough

ISBN 0 9537022 00

Acknowledgements

Acknowledgements are due to the editors of the following publications, in which some of these poems first appeared: *Bournemouth Poetry Competition Anthology, Essex Countryside, L.A.C.E. Competition Anthology, Navis, New Blackfriars, New Spokes, Orbis, Other Poetry, Quaker's Monthly, Remembered Place (An Anthology of the Houseman Society), Staple, The Interpreter's House, The English Speaking Board, The New Statesman, The North, The Observer, Use of English, Words International Anthology, Writing Women.* 'The Park' was used in Friends of the Earth's 1998 *Poems on the Buses* event. Poems have also been broadcast by BBC Radio 3 and 4.

The publishers would like to express their thanks to Peter Didsbury for his invaluable editorial help in the production of this volume.

THE CHEMISTRY
OF ANGELS

Contents

Gold Has an E-Number

A pinch emblazons exotic chocolates,
sifted fire
glitters on opulent foods.
We can eat gold.

Born in heat,
our bones and wires are part
of an architecture of sky,
like stars,
constructed from chemical meshes.

Life
must lie in the hinges,
the gaps, alchemies of exchange,
dynamic mixings.

We have power
to increase connections,
deep detritus from the universe
massed in our heads,

thoughts, ignitions;

each one of us processes
the solar system,
we add
to the recipes of moons and quarks.

Lumber

Full moon, the hills are flying
Orion like a kite,
I feel the tug of silver.

Shropshire is heavy with stars,
a fossil of ancient seas,
Long Mynd encumbered with shells,
the rigging of creatures
wrecked in rock,
lost maps of wings and fins.

The planet aslant is twisting
lava-strings, red ropes
for fliture continents,
embryo oceans
locked in ice and atoms.

My father's bones are part
of the county now,
we come from the lumber of space,
seed of light, fissions
from suns and radiations,
souls grown in chemistries
deep in the dark matter.

The little town
is weighted with lamps,
its church fixed firm as a molar.

Bending the Light

We are made from the raw
materials of space,
children of dust,
we carry reverberations,
fossilised light;
our elements never die.

Why do we navigate
life like
medieval mariners,
as if death were a ledge,
we drift
towards its rim?

Einstein in a carriage,
puzzled if passing trains
were moving or still,
discovered New Worlds,
saw the weight of the Earth
bending light.

Our perceptions
are always suspect,
who would care to deny
anti-matter
or the chemistry of angels?

Engineering

Stars:

not set like necklaces
or brooches,
not pulsing quietly
through atmospheric velvets,
chiffons of mist,

ROARING.

If there is a music of
the spheres,
it's heavy-metal,
howling ingots of sound
ripping
textures of the firmament.

Not free-wheeling;

these behemoths of space
follow patterns
laid by laws
not invented by man;

krakens of light and dark
penned into
fireballs, cosmic clouds, pits,

fix a kind
of harvest - a leaf a child, love.

On Visiting a Natural History Museum

Will superior beings preserve us in glass,
spread the pretty colours of our hair,
while at our side those televisions pass

for pets? Will we be laid out in the mass,
shown to the young who've acquired a questionnaire,
will superior beings preserve us in glass?

Will we be naked or clothed between rails of brass,
in graded shades like butterflies in the glare,
while at our sides those televisions pass

for companions? Outside offspring will sit on grass,
discuss how well we're stuffed, each specimen rare.
Will superior beings preserve us? In glass

our pigments could be stunning, if everyone has
eyelids propped open, irises ranged in a stare,
while at our sides those televisions pass

for keepers. Admired by creatures from space, alas,
we were unwary, proclaimed our planet was there.
Will superior beings preserve us in glass,
while aged aliens enter free with a pass?

Solstice

Glass bones in the wind,
the garden
cut from snow, is sketched in charcoal,
sooty prints
on the silver birch,
X rays of trees.

I'm caught behind panes,
ribs fretted
like staves in leaves,
architraves
buttressing creation
evolved
from dissolutions.

Sun rises solid
as amber,
sap squeezed from
ancient galaxies
fossilised rays constructed
from old radiations;

planets held
like sea-anemones
in an antique nugget of sky.

Plasma

The cathedral has fossils
of sea-creatures in its walls,
these stones
have been under water,
unimagined fish
have swum through this skin.

I stand in a shell of rock
holding my ear
to echoes from long-dead oceans
waves trapped
in acanthus leaves,
seabeds carved in a rose window.

Marble in floor and arcade
have come from earth's core,
steps hewn from the sun,
pillars and buttresses
sprung out of supernovas.

Moon and stars have bloomed
into people and church
which claims the final alchemy.
God meeting us
in the radiations of prayer.
Love unsettling dust.

Long Mynd

Wallflowers: scent so thick
it barricades the path
breaks against skin
like brick-dust.

Gold rolls down streets,
we walk
through solar ignitions
ashes of light
breathe the soft conflagration
of roses.

All day above Long Mynd
gliders spin
like ping-pong balls
on fountains of air,
people crowd the place
as a fair
for a go on the helter-skelters
of grass,
a view of the sky.

Prehistories
sift through the landscape,
cloud-shadows, ghosts,
amalgam from star-collisions,
stones from
the cliffs of space,
quantum phantasmagoria
that evolved
to a moon, a planet, a child.

Oriental Dress

Fog
lets slip the huge,
orange disc
of a Chinese-lantern sun.

Loosed behind trees,
watered silk
marked by the weave
of winter twigs,
in a paper garden
torn by a fence at the edge.

Such chrysanthemum light,
dissolution,
slow rending of seams,

deceives
the oriental girl
in her blazer and tie,
on her silver walk to school,

she is sheathed in
dissembling ambers.

Mrs Siu's Necklace

A single stone,
unengraved with flowers,
fruit or dragon,
nothing permitted
to incise its light.

A green sun
that has swallowed
its planets,
a jewel
that drowns the watcher;
for aeons
I swam in its depths,
drank the dark.

Jade:
a symbol of strength,
immutability,

contains
like Arctic ice

an ocean in its heart.

Chinese Wedding

Red lanterns, dragons en passant,
the room blooms scarlet,
gold, magnificence summoned.

Amber glazes, sea-creatures
glutinous and pearled
slide the throat's slope,
rice plump with
sweetcorn and peppers.

Small girls are Victorian posies,
I sit in my Chinese dress,
(a gift, black silk embroidered
with lilies in apricot and ivory),
recalling the bride as a schoolgirl,
Yu Yee braving western faces,
engraved with her first winter;

Bright Jade now encrusted
in white satin,
crinoline fraught with frills;
exchanging the ceremonial tea.

The Headmistress

Her crenellated hair
rose solidly
above a stony front,
the knitted architecture
of her dress
impressed with pillared cable,
stitches sprang
the awesome buttress of her chest.

She had made a fortress
of flesh,
each cell adhered
to the castle's code,
kept watch
against an unnamed foe.

Were the rooms
behind that impregnable brow
ever hung with silk?

The light in her windows
usually glinted
on arrows,
was it all drills and duties
or was there
occasional entertainment;
swigs of ale
from a keg of beer?

The Hunger

Please do not erase me
with your smile.

Do not diminish me
with that particular kind
of gift
that comes
from a lucky dip.

You do
have plumper cushions,
a fat house,
your roses are more succulent,
your carpets fluffier
and towels
preen themselves
on the bathroom rail.

You have holidays
in Rio,
your children sparkle
like preserves more sweetly
in your larder.

Now you've iced me with
your cakes,
leave my sugars,

I am almost down to the bone.

Hill Farmer

A tempered voice: it slices clean
as a spade,
elemental roots
from British, Saxon, Old Norse.

A Jason, at war with crops
of bracken, thistles,
dragon-seed undermining walls,
laying ambush
to his fleece of wheat;
our history weathered back,
ultimate rock,
hands obstinate as lichen.

His wife survives like the heather,
sustains purple,
is diligent with bees;
brews wine and remedies from
flowers and herbs,
stirs their concoctions
of stored sky, fermented rain;
conjurations lured from the moor,
distillations, like us, from the planet.

Being Drawn

)

Hair piled like fruit,
grapes of curls,
rich, morello ringlets;
she applied creams
blending rose and lavender
chose a necklace
with tones
of lilac and iris.

It was bearable at first,
gaze no worse than
a doctor's,
sounds of sketching
soothing as dried grasses.

Soon it became intrusive,
exposure of bones,
rifts, depths in a landscape,
the pencil digging.

Finally it hurt:
that peeling of skins
as if she were mummified,
revealing secrets
from many, little deaths.

She left,
reduced to strings
and tendons,
contained in canopic pigments,
eviscerated, drawn.

Greenhouse Effects

Strange plants hiss from corners, leaves grow fur.
Shelves of coloured suns are cocooned in heat;
seeds bloom inside his head, begin to stir

like a science-fiction tale. He loves the burr
of his own jungle created near a street.
Strange plants hiss from corners, leaves grow fur.

He is a hothouse addict and will inter
chrysanthemums for tigers in concrete,
seeds bloom inside his head, begin to stir.

The child next door is afraid: She keeps it under
her tongue that some flowers hint at sculptured meat.
Strange plants hiss. From corners, leaves grow fur

and heads with petalled scalps are sinister,
he may put one on a plate for her to eat.
Seeds bloom inside his head, begin to stir.

She'll not go back, buds could begin to purr
and little shoots start clawing at her feet.
Strange plants hiss from corners, leaves grow fur,
seeds bloom inside his head, begin to stir.

Anonymous Caller

Catalogue colours:
toffee, ecru and candy,
bracelet matching earrings,
face hard
as sugared almonds.

Sharp little smiles bite
open her mouth,
she glitters with
venomous virtue, brittle fears.

Like Hamlet's uncle
drops poison,
in one ear - creates a ghost.

Mirrors

An aviary of dresses
alive with silk
roosts on
the rail of your wardrobe.

Each day you disturb
the flock,
shake out a flight
of fabrics.

It's your own rainforest,
mimic plumage
from shops,
your several selves,
crimson macaw, blue-foot
booby, albatross

looping the world.

Bullfight

Black bull
draped in scarlet,
caparisoned in blood,
rich fold on fold rolling
over his back,
thick torrent of silk.

Taut
in his suit of lights,
the sun
a medal pinned
to his chest,
the matador's embroidered
steps belied
his skill with the sword,
he was brave,

inept.

The bull's legs cracked
with the weight
of dying,
he splintered slowly
like wood.

Each swirl of the cape
was an incantation,
power to compel the god
of the underworld;

a celebration

of life
by conjuring death.

New Manager

No fur:
not a wolf or a fox.

Limbs thin as knives,
he flicks about in his chair,
a lean machine.

He cuts:

severs heads so swiftly
each stays in place
till the victim reaches home.

His room is bloodless.

Awards Ceremony

Voices chink
among the confectionery,
dry as gin.

People are
ambushed by little biscuits,
tongue-tripped
by vol-au-vents stuffed with
shrimps and chives;

skewered on smiles.

Long-stemmed on heels,
the hostess
stands crystallised in satin,
earrings chime
in frosted silver,
contenders arranged like sweets.

There's a hint
of icebergs floating;

a glaze
from pretty, pink manners,
sensation of crockery
balanced above each head,

a sword
of Damocles fashioned from china.

Care

A supervised library visit,
women and men flutter
and chirr,
elated to seek
the brightness of books,
take one home

One man strokes his choice
like a pigeon,
caresses its plumage,
tenderness in his touch
as if something alive and trusting
pulsed in his hands.

Humbled, I turn
to my casually-handled pile
with alerted fingers,
illumined by his openness of care.

Blood-Head

A head shaped from frozen
human blood shown
by Saatchi & Saatchi.

The woman on the radio
says it isn't red,
there are globules
that slip
into scarlet.

For days I've been haunted
by the grazed head
of the toddler
murdered by boys

and now this icon,

its dislocations from pity
and grief,
spilled blood
another kind of plasticine.

I await
the high-carat penis cut
from human urine;

the ultimate golden boy.

Walking the Tiger

Home can be
the most dangerous place
in the world;

trailing flex
in a conversation plugged
into love,

boiling rage
with its handle turned t
o the baby.

She was safe as Gretel
in the gingerbread house,
silences stalked
the rooms like tigers,
walls were
hung with fearsome smiles
and worst of all,

the gifts
that looked like sweets.

★

Her sister's rage was hidden,
she sharpened
blades in the dark,
conjured dragons to fight
the incantations of
the baby.

Love
had the fiercest forging,
every endearment
given an edge.

She learned
to curdle the milk of stories,
dug pits
of fear at bedtime,
saw herself
as hero in her own epic
righting the wrong of a birth.

★

"What is the darkness mother,
Why is there night in my head?"

"The sun is shining daughter,
It's fancies that you dread."

"What are the whispers mother,
What is the blood on the bed,
And why do I feel my sister steal
Your love that should be my bread?"

"It's your evil heart my daughter,
Your sister is loving and true."

"Then why does she smile my mother,
When I cry and come to you?"

★

Barbed-wire rain rolls
down the hill,
catches my face
as I climb to your house.

Gardens
are mined with autumn,
tripwires of scent
from your favourite flower
tumble me back
to the child who gave you
unwanted blooms;
the bones
of my sister's smile
still hang in my head.

There are dark growths
between us,
seeds have swelled grief.
I know now,
your look of someone
about to be shot
was there
before I was born.

Today
I'm not laden with flowers,
bear fruit;

I am your apple, your plum.

Snow-Queen

That winter
snow reconstructed maps,
no roads, no railings,
trees were cut to their knees.

Overnight
children grew into giants,
could reach
the roofs of houses.

She walked on hedges,
huge with delight till she thrust
her foot down a bush,
perched like
a bird in crystal roots.
It was life in a storybook,
ice-bees in the wind,
she feared the White Witch.

How could she know
fairy-tales grow in the home,
the splinter of ice
is lodged in more than one heart?

Though a place may wait
by the fire,
logs spit gold;
tongues hang red icicles,

love starves like a wolf.

Named

Wild violets: unique in our
hessian garden with its rough
mats, helium roses.

Not cut like pansies
from the thick fabric of dusk;
thin panes of light, blue rain.

I know some bird has shot seeds,
yet kneel to the purple hassock,
for me they are runes.

Named for this flower,
my mother died this spring,
though we were not estranged,
words were often oblique;

I need such visitations.

Outlast

Bridge smudged to a ghost
as the Severn shape-shifts into mist,
river occluded to nimbus and mica.

Muted hawsers, pillars hung in clouds,
we move through dissolutions
afloat on piles of colours,
steel and tarmac
mutated to charcoal and ash.

Grief draws us north like a rope
to the hulk of the church,
so old it has anchored an iceberg
of cold within walls,
that yields
to the focus of faces and lamps.

Prayers older than the nave
come in with the mirror wood
of the coffin. My mother at ninety,
hidden in death as she was in life,
when she stacked silence,
her needs more heavy than rock.

This place is hewn, stands
through strength of mason, monk,
fierceness of faith
stiffened by warrior-code
that will outlast the tower sinking
into the hill, Long Mynd;
ark of belief
more elemental than planets.

The Learning

Hyacinths are not fragile,
these petals curve solid flesh.

Perfume lurks like a bruise
rendering the room unsafe.

Sweetness heavy as headaches,
those afternoons
with grandma and her friend,
ruffles of skin at wrist and throat,
ash in their voices,
whispers flew
from papery mouths like moths.

She remembered rings and brooches,
teacups that alighted,
a flock of china, delicate bones,
spoons spread like quills.

Alone, inconsequential,
she had faded into the furniture,
absorbed the confectionery of deceit
the art of diffusion into a landscape.

Gift for Josette

Perfumes release their top notes
like divas,
vie with extracts, essences,
musks and dusks,
green acridities from herbs, leaves;
violets, geraniums, hush of lilac.

Not these,
nor tendernesses in velvet.
We elude scarves and brooches,
littered sequins, beads.

Not cut-crystal with light
as an artefact,
a weight, an encrustation
to be carried in dishes of glitter.

This bowl remains unresolved,
a conjuration,
warp in space and time,
a wraith unfixed in future or past,
time-machine coming or going.

The glassblower has summoned
a twist in air,
ice-mouth spun from a single swirl
till the owner translates its breath.

Birth

Pines on the moor,
huge vertebrae in snow,
nothing is more lonely
than the signpost,
final bone of a lost tribe?

Unafraid, dark-faced
and curious,
sheep bulk through mist,
creatures from an Ice-Age,
solid as packed fog,
carved rugs
dropping ice at fringes.

Legs frail as charcoal,
they crack
the frozen spines of streams,
strike delicate chinks
from paths of stopped sky.

We take the dog home.

Dark flies its crows,
frost blackens;
from such stone wombs
some lamb
will slacken and cry.

Spiders

(on learning they went into space on a shuttle)

It's their run that alarms,

that swift
articulation of many legs
implies total brain
hung between
complex scaffolding
how else could they control
such architecture,
such balances and loadings
on those threads?

I can cope with
the special relativity of cats,
whatever direction they fall,
the ground
lands on their feet,

(as Einstein said
"Does Oxford stop at this station?")

Spiders are suspect,
have too much mastery
of the air-waves,
swinging through time,
can solve too many equations
at a sling of a limb

In deep sky
they lost focus,

warp and weft were dislocated;
mathematicians sometimes unhinge
with their connections,
when nowhere is upside-down,
where do new webs begin?

We need an earth or a sun,
a faith or belief
to give displacement in space
a tug in the dark.

Belonging

Frogspawn hefted in fist;
mouth fixed,
he hoisted
the glass of living eyes
bubbles massed
like his own saliva
that would not free his tongue.

Quests
into green darknesses,
emerald pits,
where nettles hissed from
the undergrowth,
shadows flicked black flames,
pools weighted with light
tolled sky,
went beyond words.

He too had tribute,
gifts he'd guard with steel
of fealty,
release as frogs.

The class
stilled to the glitter
of quiet,
sworn sword of his arm.

Owl

His face is concave
to focus sound,

a radio-telescope
in quills,
the countenance of radar.

Each feather
is silent as a moth,
his body
stuffed with wool and fur,
a lover of soft coats
lined in scarlet,

a flying wardrobe
with hooks.

His call hangs
full-moon on branches.

He's round,
a tea-cosy ribbed
in white, grey and brown.

Who could believe
his needles knit blood?

Cows

They drink the stream,
hefty tongues
looping long slivers of sky,
swallowing clouds
and trees,
slurping the landscape.

Their muscles are boulders
under the skin
if hills had mobile kith
they would look
like cattle
with promontories and outcrops;
walking cliffs.

Cows are mathematical;
the massive calculation
of their moves,
their weights and pendulums,
great engines
fuelled by grass and rain.

They stand like giant toys
cast in the minerals
of the afternoon,
wait to be put
to bed in wooden boxes.

Their vulnerability hurts
the way they accept
metal mouths,
the ultimate suckers.

The sun is iron ore
on their flanks,
each cow with a chain
of stomachs
fills its leather buckets
with silver,
sways them back to water-meadows,
begins the alchemy of milk.

Dog

He digs
for odours like truffles,
moves through
rainbows of scents;

a walking pomander,

head stuffed
with luscious leaks from dumps,
old stumps of sheds
and gardens,

trailing
his special perfume
with the aplomb of a matador's cape
or feather boa.

He's a mower for
any stink,
flaunts the smell of fish
for a waistcoat,
fat for cummerbund of cat.

Coming back
from rambles he's burred
with pungencies,
fumy seeds and hooks,

traced with
the neighbourhood's contours,

he's the local, olfactory map.

Sound of the Dinosaurs

Some had crests of bone filled
with tubes of air like trombones.

Perhaps saurian blues,
(pure as a hunting horn or trumpets of
Tutankhamun),
pulsed giant ferns, green deeps
under grasses the size of oaks,
dark currents in succulent seas.

We can find no fossils of sound,
no music trapped in stone or amber,
extract no stomp
entombed in ice at the Poles.

I mourn those notes blown
through earth's antique landscape,
released into space, now traversing
the dark matter to the waiting spheres.

Last Outing

Sun ruinous, tindery,
a wicker landscape brittle
with old gold
frayed into threads.

Dry stalks
and aromatic dusts,
your body light as straw,
poppies turning
to rust and cinnamon,
we walked
like paper people.

I searched
for a place to rest your
tearing silks;
a man and woman faded
from their bench,
they had seen your face,
already a leaf
afloat on its strings
looking at kites tug sky.

"I saw them once more".
Your voice
was not powdery or dry,
but round
and satisfactory as an apple.

Gift

He lifted her.

Brittle, wasted
within,
she was raised
like someone drowned
breaking through
the ice
of her body,

frost
cracking under skin,

waterfall hands.

The man was a tree.
She splintered
on his bones.
He wore
her like a crucifixion.

What they had been
redeemed

the gift of grief.

Witness

Your look
caught from the retina,
sun turned black,

voice,
soundwaves
with hidden undertow.

You had
fought this illness once
and won.

Now we knew
there were no words,
this time
you would not be able
to cry
and I, a witness,
would circumnavigate oceans,

an albatross

trailing
waters like the moon
dragging the sea.

★

Interrogation
by liquids and screens,

life sharpened
with needles,

your belly
a scarlet nest,
they took out growths,
wrapped
you in tin-foil.

It was cold
on the high mountain bed.

     ★

Skin
clipped with thirty
silver fish-bones
withdrawn
without anaesthetic.

And still there were stitches,

you feared
one nurse who removed them
like nails.

"Do you want to take them home?"

You stapled a smile.

      ★

Grief
is heavy as masonry,
shoulders slung,
bones turning to stone.

It is hard
to move my feet,
my hands are hewn.

I am kin
to those sculptures
emerging from rock
or settling

back to the planet.

★

The chocolate are hand-made,
miniature carvings
presented in pleated gold
under paper glass.

More fragile than china,
I carry them
desperately on the bus
as if they could save your life.

Transfusion of roses
on your locker,
I know you want to speak
about grief,
release me from its trap
like some small animal,
you fear I will
bite through a limb

We talk of tea and biscuits,
covers on the bed,
your cats, the muted sun.
White blooms of cloud
hold back the unravelling sky;

we swop
our friendship like plasma.

★

Face
set sail
towards infinities.

Death, a ruinous sun,
burns against bone,
your body a ship,
fibres pulled by tides.

Each day
frays a little
like rope,

we give
you freight of love.

Incision

Death
has moved in with me;

I saw
its shadow adjust
to my shape,
slip into my skin.

I am brought
to a pure place;

the blade is clean,
it is beautiful,
blood will
rise like flame
to the frost of the knife.

The doctor's look
is honed,
it has been engineered
to the rim,

precision
has sharpened his hands.

I recall
how Amazon women
were rumoured to cut off
one breast,
the better to carry
their weapons;

I am a fighting-woman.

Prognosis

X rays, confrontations
with worlds
we carry unseen,
craters in thoughts,
landscapes remote
as the moons of Jupiter.

We wait
with clustered ghosts,
mother, sister, uncle, friend,
teacher, nurse,
the man in the bank,
we trail their voices,
carry their
clamps and benedictions.

Our hidden choirs
disrupt the body's hydraulics,
manipulate the physics
in our blood; though chemicals speak
in charts, tubes,
phantoms haunt the response;

infiltrate plasma.

Spores

St Luke's little summer;
the sun
a golden blizzard,

at the nature reserve
in Epping Forest
I buy postcards of fly agaric,
the toxic mushroom
crimson skin
pricked with white.

Some fungi fire
their seeds like cannon,
the spores from one
could double
the weight of the world.

Did they come from stars,
ride in
on meteorites,
sleeping gun at the hip?

They could hibernate
for centuries,
emerge in scarlet craniums;
poised to tick.

I recall the fearsome growth
in your head,
how after your death,
I sat under trees
received their radiation
like green rain.

Red Shift

Light slams;
there's a hospital din.

He dives into darkness.
Pain holds him
upside down by the leg,
hauls him back on a red rope.

He stares at his screaming limb,
the nurse has a cumulus smile
and thorny hands.

There's a white block
weighing him down.
It flowers.
His foot is a poppy of flame.

Why is the window so calm?
Why is the chair not burning?

He swings in a spectrum-shift
suspended on voices,
revolving in new dimensions
sprung through the prism of pain.

When his body unwinds,
he knows there are colours
he's never entered,
retains an inner refraction;

red shift
through circuits within.

Angels Come to Church Stretton

It was night:

the angels climbed Helmeth
chatting in twos and threes
like walkers coming to call
for a guest.

Radiance interleaved the dark
as if overcoats quelled their light,
ambience muted,
no harps, no fierce quills.

A few bent over the bed,
others went on talking,
an event diffuse and tender
rather than holy.

I strove to make myself seen.
I'd become a wraith,
a ghost
who clung to the wall.

Later, odd bits of music
floated like feathers;
a friend said it was trauma,
biochemistry - due to a death?

Intimations

Cats almost imperceptibly
thicken night, no creature ever
possesses its landscape more.
We pour out moons of milk
for their delight.

Nor can we tell them of death
for they are quite impervious
to the words that build such awe;
we meet but do not mingle
in our plight.

Which leads to presences
uncomprehended, bright postulation
of angels opening a door.
Do we drink, not questioning
their bowls of light?

Much Wenlock Priory

Wind blows through
ruined arches stealing
their dust,
motes from chancel and nave
float across fields,
are embedded in fence
and fleece,
adhere to skin
and blades of grass,
are breathed in the air.

Shropshire takes back
its stone,
hills are infiltrated
by strange foliage,
chiselled acanthus leaves,
embossed vine.

Slowly
sheep inhale pillars
and walls,
corn absorbs old carvings
rocks assimilate the
lancet window.

Streams take in atoms from
buttress and font;
sky crumbles.

Peat Bog

It builds like a reef
of black coral,
bodies of sphagnum moss,
plants that pack rain.

Pressed to black butter
at its base,
so smooth it would spread
on bread,
its living skin
has shoals of insects,
dragonfly, damsel,
wings iridescent as fins,
saurian green.

It quakes if you jump;
swallowed a farmer
with horse and cart
its harvest, black fires
dried to bricks.

It can feed its own,
this monstrous
whale of the landscape
wallowing for ten millennia,
blowing inexorable gases,
holding its ground.

Reflections

Umbrellas
open at bus-stops,
instant herbaceous borders.

Silk
slings along streets,
long, bright bales unreel
under wheels.

Shop-windows splash
at our feet,
we walk on
reflected coats,
break panes of sky.

The town
stretches its skins.

Surrounded by mirrors,
I'm aware
for the first time
of my heart on the other side
of the glass,

wiring reversed like
Mr Spock;

new being buried in light.

The Plant

At first it was unassuming,
two small leaves inflated slowly.

Overnight it rampaged,
in one week swallowed the fence,
leaped and licked
like Jack's beanstalk.

The gardener was enslaved,
a pail in each hand,
he was the sorcerer's apprentice.

This was his own, green beast,
it clamoured and hissed,
shot out new claws and tongues,
grabbed watering-cans
at a gulp; took over.

The gardener's wife watched
her husband's arms wear to sticks,
he flickered in moonlight,
silver weights at his wrists.

She heard the tick in seeds,
the seething; knew we always
have a need to feed
what can never be slaked.

Rain

There's an art
in listening to rain.

It has its own topography,
contours of rhythm
make maps,
hushed precipice of trees,
fanfare paths.

The Chinese had a rain-pavilion,
a place for watching
frayed silver
embroidered with leaves
and birds
falling silk scissored
by wind
among living pagodas.

The garden emerges
in soundwaves,
strings of sky profile
the slope of grass,
small gaps,
where lichens trace
their sonar along the wall.

The Western

Rocks
rubbed by brass
winds evolved across
millennia.
Sound-prints in stacks,
strata from
different carats of sun,
soft-structures
eaten away,
the core stuff.
Sounds
are simple,
coyotes, owls, hooves
at night,
a howling moon.
Cacti
rise huge, armorial,
illusion of mist
from fires, horses, guns,
gold like blood,
love in a bone-climate.

The Park

Voices
grow tall,
flying like paper kites
over grass,
trailing the children.

Old ladies
talk among the embroidery
of flowers,
delight in loops and knots,
threads of doubt,
pauses for perspectives
to stitch light.

Dogs chat

and babies
ride in silver palaces,
reach for baubles

of sun and lake and sky.

New Housing Estate

Raw houses,
bricks the colour of ham,
uncorked babies
dusted with light reach
for pieces of sun
that spill
through naked fences.

Flowerbeds lie crusted
as old chests
crammed with sufficient gold
for a king's ransom.

Thistles
cling to corners,
muggers alert
for a break in the wall.

It's a place seeking roots,
hooked by a couple
of roads
to the edge of town,
loneliness
stretches at night
like the hawsers of rope.

Freight

We walk inside the green bowl
of the park
engraved with lake and trees;
a huge, glass ball
blown warm with summer,
thick with the smoke of roses.
Leaves become sails
stitched with sky,
we fly through the afternoon
with a cargo of flowers
and paper kites.
Babies laugh
from the portholes of prams
and old men sleep
their ropes coiled down.
We anchor at dusk
and loaded with sunlight,
disembark.

Change in the Light

Wind smudges soft graphites
into the lake. Silver cleaves.

Corners in rooms will sleep
all day, absences
take shape, mass fur.

The park playground creates
its own incandescence,
full sun of the roundabout,
meteoric slides,
red swings for lamps.

Amy's delight is muted, she holds
the weight of play gravely.
As she swings and spins,
we speak about grief
and as the colours go out,
sun conjures the ghost
of a moon, tips the world.

We slip behind shadows;
life is a hall of mirrors,
one step can reveal refractions
or the back of the glass,
shift negatives in the light.

Script

No snow:

I mark the black
and white calligraphy
of the garden
drawn by invisible
Chinese brushes
weighted with frost.

Ultimate script
unsolved,
inlaid with ghosts
of flowers, leaves,
shadows of vertebrae
not yet achieved;

matrix of angels?

Life
folded like fans
releases
its landscapes slowly.

Reverberations

The tree is ringing;

its cage of massive frost
has split
in the sudden sun,
every branch hums.

The Chinese
boys learning English
don't believe
my tale about music.

I send
them to stand under
silver rigging;
heads poised like radar,
they catch
bright hoops from soundwaves,

rebound astonished
at schists of notes
refracting
through bones;

a birch-tree singing.